HOMESTUDY BOOT CAMP

MONICA A. JONES, M.S.W.

COPYRIGHT

Homestudy Boot Camp, Copyright ©2013 by Simply Managed. All rights reserved. Printed in the United States of America. No part of this book may be copied, stored, reproduced or used in any manner whatsoever without written permission from the author. Violators will be prosecuted to the fullest extent of the law. For information contact us at info@homestudybootcamp.com.

This publication is designed to provide accurate and authoritative information in regard to the subject matter covered. It is sold with the understanding that neither the author nor the publisher is engaged in rendering legal, financial, investment, accounting, psychological or other professional services. If legal, financial, investment, accounting, psychological or other expert professional assistance is desired or required, the services of a competent professional in the applicable field should be sought.

CONTENTS

The author has gone to great lengths to ensure the accuracy and relevancy of the contents in this book. In general the contents of this book can be relied upon for accurate and applicable information on the covered topics. However due to various state laws and unique circumstances, no guarantee, promises or accuracy stipulations are being made as to any particular result or outcome. Individuals must adhere to all applicable state rules, regulations and laws.

CREATIVITY

The publisher is solely responsible for publishing. Otherwise, the ultimate design, concept, editorial accuracy and views expressed or implied in this work are those of the author.

Copyright © 2013 Monica A. Jones, M.S.W.

All rights reserved.

ISBN:-13: 978-0615830179
ISBN-10: 061583017X

DEDICATION

I thank God for giving me the creativity to complete this book.

To my wonderful husband Les, you are a major factor in this work coming forth. I love you and I am forever grateful for your selflessness, encouragement and commitment.

To my beautiful son Jonathan Noah, you are the inspiration for this book. Each time I see your face, I'm reminded of the unconditional love that you give, and the joy that you bring to our lives. I want other people to be blessed with a baby just like you.

CONTENTS

1 **Why This Book Was Written**   1

The ultimate insider's guide to the adoption homestudy

2 **So, What's A Homestudy Anyway?**   4

From the bedroom to the bank account: A detailed look into what they're going to ask you and how to give effective responses

3 **All Interviews Are Not Created Equal**   41

The appointment you must be prepared for

4 **The Paper Trail**   48

Breeze through the additional paperwork associated with the homestudy

5 **Approved To Adopt! Or Not**   65

"Problem Approvals" and the most common reasons applicants are disqualified from adopting

6 **The Vault**   73

Comments, advice and the secret thoughts of experienced adoption assessors: What they really think about adoptive applicants

Homestudy and Adoption Definitions   80

Frequently Asked Questions   85

WHAT YOU'RE NOT SUPPOSED TO KNOW...

1 WHY THIS BOOK WAS WRITTEN

The ultimate insider's guide to the adoption homestudy

Homestudy Boot Camp is the only book written by an adoption assessor, which equips prospective parents with "inside information" to make the homestudy process easier.

Before anyone can adopt they must complete and pass an adoption homestudy. Far too often would be adoptive parents panic over the homestudy process. They're anxious because they don't know what to expect, and they are afraid of failure. Prospective parents have long needed a no stress, no guess method to prepare for their homestudy.

If only people knew the questions they would be asked, what to avoid saying and what their adoption assessor *really* thought about them, they would be better prepared for this process. Thanks to Homestudy Boot Camp the wait is over! Homestudy Boot Camp goes deep into the homestudy process, as well as the minds of the adoption assessors who complete the homestudies. You will learn exactly what to expect, what questions are coming your way, and the absolute best way to respond!

Our Approach:

Homestudy Boot Camp is filled with six "tricks of the trade" chapters designed to reduce anxiety and boost your confidence to complete your homestudy effortlessly.

What This Book Does:

- Puts your mind at ease by knowing exactly what to expect during the homestudy process

- Teaches you the Do's and the Don'ts during the homestudy
- Goes inside the minds of experienced adoption assessors to bring you uncut information
- Dissects the homestudy line by line to extract the most relevant items crucial to your success
- Discusses the things that most people aren't willing to admit or talk about
- Provides guidance on answering deeply personal questions without feeling vulnerable
- Prevents you from wondering if you've given answers that will disqualify you from adopting
- Teaches you how to avoid giving answers that send up red flags in the mind of the adoption assessor
- Discloses the top reasons applicants are denied the opportunity to adopt
- Provides information on what happens after you've been approved to adopt
- Pinpoints obstacles that prevent you from being chosen by stakeholders

What This Book Does Not Do:

- Give shortcuts to pass the homestudy:

    You'll still have to jump through the same hoops as everyone else. However you'll be prepared for sweatless victory

- Guarantee that regardless of your situation you will be approved to adopt:

    However we'll show you how to significantly improve your chances of being approved to adopt

- Guarantee that a stakeholder will pick you to become an adoptive parent:

    *However we can show you how to increase your chances
    of standing out in a sea of adoptive applicants,
    to increase your chances of being chosen to adopt*

- Show you how to avoid answering deeply personal question:

    *But we will show you how to answer them in a way that
    makes you feel less vulnerable, and gives your
    adoption assessor the information they need to write a
    great homestudy on your behalf*

Homestudy Boot Camp promises to be an invaluable tool to assist you in preparing for your homestudy. Utilizing straight forward discussions, practical advice and a little candid humor, expect our Boot Camp to whip you into shape quickly for the experience of a lifetime! So, without further delay, let's dive in!

2 SO, WHAT'S A HOMESTUDY ANYWAY

*From the bedroom to the bank account:
A detailed look into what they're going to ask you and how to give effective responses*

Congratulations on your decision to adopt! The first step in your journey to adopting a child is to locate a licensed adoption agency that you feel comfortable working with. This agency will require you to fill out an "adoption application" or an "application for child placement." Once your application is processed, you will be contacted to complete a "homestudy assessment." The outcome of the homestudy will determine if you will be approved or denied to adopt.

A homestudy is an assessment of your family and your readiness to adopt. Your readiness to adopt is determined based on a comprehensive review of your life experiences, health, lifestyle, extended family relationships, attitudes, support system, values, beliefs, and other factors relating to the prospective adoption. This information is then summarized in an adoption homestudy report. Once the homestudy is completed the professional completing your homestudy will either approve or deny you to become an adoptive parent.

No one can adopt without an approved homestudy. (Chapter 5 discusses why applicants are denied the opportunity to adopt.) Depending on the state you live in, the title and training of the professional completing your homestudy will vary. Following are some examples of the titles and educational backgrounds of such person: adoption assessor, homestudy assessor, adoption case worker, adoption case manager, adoption counselor, homestudy coordinator and homestudy counselor. This professional usually has a degree and/or experience in social work, casework, counseling, marriage and family therapy, community counseling, adoption counseling, or child development. For the purpose of this book we refer to this professional as the adoption assessor – as this is the most widely used title. Regardless of which title your adoption assessor holds, due to state requirements, you can be assured that this person is significantly qualified, well trained and highly educated as it pertains to adoption and homestudy matters.

The homestudy is very important and multi functional. In one regard the homestudy serves as a document that the birthparent or an adoption placement worker (known as stakeholders) reviews to choose a family for a child. Please note that if a birthparent requests to see your homestudy your personal identifying information will be withheld from them to protect your identity.

In the second regard, excerpts from the homestudy can be used for the hard bound or electronic profile adoptive parents will set up - post homestudy approval - to market themselves to birthparents.

Given the importance of the homestudy it's vitally important to provide your adoption assessor with substantive information in which they can use to write your homestudy in a way that "sells" you to the stakeholder. Of course there are standard questions that your adoption assessor will ask you. However I will give you advice on how to be proactive with the information you supply, as to set yourself apart from your "competitors" (other homestudies being considered the same time as yours.)

While the average adoption assessor writing a homestudy has learned to write creatively, they must be supplied with information they can work with. Your adoption assessor will not make false statements on your behalf, but with a little creative writing they can take your story from blah to ahhh!

Following is every topic in the homestudy, along with "insider tips" detailing how to answer the questions to produce a competitive homestudy!

Transportation:

How many vehicles do you own? Can you provide proof of insurance? Do you own any recreational vehicles or motorcycles? Are your modes of transportation in running condition? If you do not have a vehicle then you will need to demonstrate alternative access to transportation such as living close to a bus line, etc. The adoption assessor will want to verify that you have automobile insurance. If you do not already have infant/child car seats your adoption assessor can document "will obtain" on your homestudy and this will be completely acceptable.

Want to make a great impression on a stakeholder? Go ahead and purchase an age appropriate car seat and have your adoption assessor indicate you have done this. This move reflects that you are motivated more than the average applicant to become a parent. Your assessor can write something along the lines of "Mr. and Mrs. Applicant are so motivated to adopt that they have already purchased an age appropriate car seat to prepare for their child. This makes you stand out amongst a sea of competitive applicants because the average applicant does not do this, as they are advised to wait to purchase a car seat after they have been chosen by a stakeholder. This approach can only work to your advantage if you know for sure what age range you are adopting. If you are open to adopting ages 0-10 this method cannot work because the range is too wide to purchase a car seat. However if you are absolutely sure that you want to adopt a particular age (such as a newborn or a toddler) then this is a great strategy!

Military History :

Each applicant will need to list any military history that they have. If you are no longer in the military be prepared to discuss the type of discharge you received. If it's anything other than honorable you will want to explain what occurred and what you have done to overcome it. While it's understandable that things happen – stakeholders will want to know that you have made attempts to address the less than honorable discharge. If you have a difficult time articulating this, speak with your adoption assessor for ideas.

If you provide them with the information they'll figure out how to make it sound impressive. If you are currently in the military that could concern some birthparents, as they may wonder if you'll be around to care for the child. Have your adoption assessor discuss how you plan on making room in your schedule to parent a child.

There was one such military couple I worked with a decade ago. The husband was in the Army reserves and had been through several deployments, each lasting at least 1 year. I was concerned that a birthparent would view this negatively, assuming that the child would not see their father often. This situation is often referred to as "absent parent dynamic."

After digging a little deeper I learned that the husband served in a Unit that had recently been inundated with volunteers, therefore decreasing the likelihood he would be called upon to travel and serve.

Based on this information I was able to document that an adopted child would not experience "absent parent dynamic." In return, we hoped this would put a birthparent at ease whose only hesitation in picking this military family was the concern over their availability.

Criminal History:

You will be required to undergo criminal record and child abuse background checks. Misdemeanors from long ago (10+ years) along with a good explanation of your behavior are usually not held against you. Felony convictions of any charge involving children or illegal substances will most likely not be allowed. (For a list of criminal convictions that will prevent you from adopting please see Chapter 5.)

It is vitally important to be honest about any criminal activity or convictions in your history. Just when you think that DUI from 20 years ago is too old to make a dent on the radar, it pops up on a criminal background check. This type of crime will not in and of itself disqualify you from adopting. However not putting this on your application could be seen as deception and deception will disqualify you from adopting.

There are different circumstances surrounding situations like this. Sometimes people flat out lie about a criminal history. Other times they truly forget about that mark they have on their record, in particular if it's old or thought to be minor. Let's take a look at the former of the two. Let's say that you really did forget about your 20 year old DUI. Maybe you were really young and made a dumb mistake and you don't even think about it anymore. Omissions of this nature will have to be discussed with your adoption agency and adoption assessor. They would question you to determine if the omission was intentional or not. If they determine the omission was intentional they will refuse to continue the homestudy process and you will be denied the opportunity to adopt. If they determine that the omission was unintentional they will likely move forward with the homestudy.

Even if you are allowed to move forward with the homestudy, your assessor is likely to mistrust you throughout the remainder of the process. Adoption assessors are called to subscribe to a particular level of professionalism, one that requires a high level of objectivity.

However adoption assessors are human and although we strive for objectivity, there is a huge amount of subjectivity in the work that we do as well. Therefore whether you intentionally or unintentionally omit criminal information two things could happen. First, your assessor will likely filter everything else you say through skeptical eyes and ears. This doesn't mean that they won't approve you for adoption. But it does mean that if you do get approved they may add some comments about your credibility in the "additional assessor observations" section. This is important as stakeholders will see this, and when you're competing with other adoptive families you don't want *anything* in your homestudy that could take you out of the running.

The second thing that could happen is if you need additional assistance during or after the homestudy process, such as a phone call made on your behalf, your assessor might put you at the bottom of their to-do list because of their personal feelings toward you. Given the consequences of intentional and unintentional omissions of criminal records, it's advisable that you go to great lengths to remember, research and dig as deep as possible to obtain this information.

Neighborhood/Community:

Be prepared to describe your environment. Do you have a relationship with your neighbors? What resources does your community offer to help you parent a special needs child? What type of neighborhood do you live in? Do you live in a safe neighborhood or a high crime area? If you live in a high crime area what plan of action do you have to ensure the safety of a child? Be familiar with and prepared to discuss the crime statistics of your neighborhood before meeting with your adoption assessor. If you have great crime statistics ask your adoption assessor to highlight this in your homestudy. Anytime you can make a truthful statement and sound impressive, you're doing yourself a favor!

What are the demographics of your community? If you are adopting a child from a different racial or cultural background you need to consider how welcoming your community would be toward them.

Although some people want to believe that the world is colorblind – it's not. And not all communities are welcoming to interracial adoption. Although it's against the law for adoption placement workers to consider race as a factor when choosing adoptive families, it's not against the law for birthparents to do so. Therefore if you are open to different races/cultures be sure to mention specifics about how your child would fit into the community where you reside. Perhaps you could discuss the diversity of the area where you live, how the community has been welcoming to other adopted children who are from different races/cultures, your willingness to educate yourself and teach your adoptive child about their race/culture, etc. If you do not live in a diverse neighborhood are you willing to move to one? This may seem drastic but due to the dynamics of interracial adoption it's necessary to consider. This sort of commitment goes a long way with birthparents that have reservations in picking you, because you are of a different race/culture than their child. Demonstrating your willingness to address cultural issues can help birthparents feel more comfortable with choosing you!

School System:

What is your school system like? Which schools would your child attend? How is your school system rated? If your district is rated excellent or excellent with distinction, mention this and ask your adoption assessor to highlight it in the homestudy. Live in a poorly performing school district? Then don't mention your school rating unless it's *painfully obvious* that your district underperforms and omitting this fact would raise questions about your credibility and openness. For example, you live in Major City X and everyone in the country knows the district associated with this city has the worst record in the nation. In this case you would need to state the obvious, followed up with your plan to ensure your child's academic success. Some of your options could be but are not limited to, moving, private school, homeschooling, utilizing tutors, after school programs, supplementing your child's education with library trips, computer software, summer school or parental instruction.

Residential History:

Ahh...here's where it can get interesting! This part of the homestudy requires that you record every residence you've held for the last 10 years. Most people are average when it comes to this in that they've had 2 or 3 residences in the last 10 years. A minority of applicants are in the "extreme" category in that they have lived in one place for the last ten years or they have a pattern of moving every other year (if they even stay around that long!).

Whichever category you fall into ensure that your assessor writes a narrative either accentuating your stable residential history, or minimizing the impact of your frequent address changes by highlighting positive reasons for the movement. This type of explanation is not standard in a homestudy. You must ask your assessor to specifically comment on this. Be proactive, as you never know when a stakeholder will raise an eyebrow to your residential history.

Employment History:

Each state requires that all adoptive applicants document their employment history. More importantly and less discussed are the conclusions drawn by stakeholders when reading about your employment history. We all know that a long and stable employment history looks great on any application. If this applies to you then by all means ask you assessor to emphasize it in your homestudy. Likewise if your employment history is sketchy or if you change jobs frequently, you may be judged as an impulsive person. I know, it's not fair! You're not impulsive – you just like sharing your awesome skills with multiple employers. Unfortunately most stakeholders will not see it this way. They will most likely perceive you as impulsive and unstable.

Don't just ignore the fact that you've had 6 jobs in the last 6 years. Stakeholders are most likely going to question your frequent job changes and your ability to provide stability for a child. In order to halt the questions before they start, following is a great way to address what adoption assessors, birthparents, and adoption placement workers are privately thinking. Ask your assessor to acknowledge the facts in the homestudy but then pivot away from it and discuss how your frequent job changes are not reflective of your ability to parent.

You could say something along the lines of, "I realize that I've held 6 jobs over the last 6 years." "I was undergoing transition in my life and it took awhile to find a career that suited me." "While I understand someone questioning my ability to be a stable parent, rest assured that my frequent job changes are in no way indicative of my ability to provide a stable environment for a child, as evidenced by the number of years I've babysat nieces, nephews, etc or volunteered in the church nursery, community center, etc." "I am now confident that I have found a career path that I can build on while continuing to provide a loving and stable home for a child." If you are self employed ask your assessor to highlight the personality, determination and fortitude that it takes to run a business.

Marital History:

This section of the homestudy discusses all legal martial relationships you've been a part of. "Legal marital relationship" is defined by your state. You will document the date the relationship started, separated and officially ended. If you have only been married once, and have a reasonably strong marriage, this section will be easy for you. However the reality is that many people have divorce, remarried and will have one or more marital relationships to list in this section. You are required to list any marital relationship you've had, whether it was short lived, annulled or a nightmare!

Most birthparents are not stable themselves and are looking for something they cannot provide their child - which is a stable loving couple in a committed relationship. Don't obsess over the fact that you may have been married more than once. What you should do is focus on the quality of the marriage you're in now. If you have had several marriages, it's a good idea to have your assessor discuss what happened in those marriages, what you learned from them and how they have made you better. Even if you have ill feelings toward your ex spouse, do not reflect this in the homestudy. This is a very competitive process, and you don't want to be ruled out because you sound bitter about your ex spouse.

Infertility issues can cause a major strain on your emotional well being, physical health and not to mention your bank account. Infertility can also impact the quality of one's marriage, especially in the areas of finance and intimacy. Many times a couple has spent significant financial resources on fertility treatments. And sometimes the process costs more than one spouse is willing to spend. Other times intimacy is affected because couples are focusing on conception more than pleasure, which can diminish the desire to engage in sex.

Because your adoption assessor may ask about this area of your marriage you will need to be prepared to discuss it. Given that adoption assessors are keenly aware of how infertility affects marriage, a red flag goes up if a couple denies that infertility has had no effect on their marriage. While it is possible that infertility has had no effect on the quality of a marriage, it is not likely. It is in your best interest to be completely open and honest about the impact infertility has had on your marriage. This is obviously an uncomfortable topic to discuss with a complete stranger. However try to keep your number one goal in mind, which is that of becoming a parent. And if it takes divulging some intimate information, even if momentarily, it will be worth it in the end.

Sometimes people attend counseling to address the emotions associated with infertility issues and sometimes they don't. Either way couples have usually engaged in some sort of processing or working through the various stages of fertility disappointment and its associated grief. Talk about how this has affected the quality of your marriage. It will help you connect with the reader of your homestudy more. If you are still dealing with infertility grief then you may want to put your homestudy on hold until you have dealt with the issue. This is not to say that you should never adopt. Nor am I suggesting that you wait to adopt until you feel 100% okay with your infertility issues. Grief and loss come in cycles and there are going to be times when you thought that you were over it and something triggers sad thoughts. However what I do suggest is that before you adopt, you should feel emotionally whole enough to care for an adopted child and your other family members. You need to ensure that the effects of your infertility are not so debilitating that you cannot perform activities of daily living.

Non-Marital Significant Relationships:

For a variety of reasons some applicants will refrain from listing non-marital significant relationships. Some believe this will make the relationship section of their application and homestudy look better, some don't believe that the relationship was significant enough to list, and others may prefer to forget that they were ever in a relationship with that person! While all of the aforementioned rationalizations are reasonable, it's imperative that you understand when to list a non-marital relationship and when not to list it. This bargaining piece only applies to "non-marital relationships."

Single applicants should still be encouraged about the homestudy and adoption process. Birthparents do choose single parents to adopt their children. But as a single person be careful about how you address your relationship status. If you are single and not involved with anyone then simply state that. However you will need to mention the role any suitor who comes into your life would play in your child's life. Birthparents need to know that you will remain committed to raising your adopted child, even after you meet Mr. or Mrs. Wonderful.

It is required by the state that you document any significant relationship you've been involved in. If you are currently in a significant relationship you will want to talk about how that person will be involved in your adopted child's life. You will also want to discuss if the relationship is headed toward marriage or not.

If a birthparent really likes your profile and is on the verge of picking you, give them more of an incentive to choose you by mentioning that your current relationship is headed toward marriage. Of course you would only state this if it's true.

You are afforded the discretion of mentioning non-significant relationships. If you only date from time to time and the person will not be around your child, then you may want to state something along the lines of "while you have gone out on a few dates, you mostly spend your free time with friends and that you are fully committed to taking care of a child." Avoid using dating descriptors such as "casual dating" "just friends" and "it's not a serious relationship." These terms and other similar ones conger up thoughts of loose and free, uncommitted and general instability. These are also relationship statuses that many birthparents themselves are in. Considering they are looking for someone in a better position than they are to parent their child, you will want to bend over backwards to avoid making them think that you are just as unstable as they are. Even if this is not true, these are often the impressions that birthparents get. Considering their opinion is what counts the most, you definitely want to avoid this language. You may be thinking that single adoptive parents have to "prove" themselves more to stakeholders than married couples. While this might be unfair, it is true to a certain degree. Be yourself, but carefully construct how you describe your relationship status.

Relationship Between Applicant #1 and Applicant #2:

If you are in a significant or martial relationship be prepared to discuss: when you met, how you met, your courtship activities, why you decided to get married, why you have not married up to this point, the reaction from family and friends regarding your relationship and/or engagement, activities you enjoyed when you dated and activities you enjoy as a married couple. If you have gone on any particularly rare or fun vacations you may want to talk about that. Describe yourself doing routine things, as well as exciting and eventful things.

You will be asked about who handles specific functions within the household such as cooking, cleaning, laundry, yard work and paying bills. You will be asked about your communication style, how you resolve disagreements, and how you plan to keep your relationship strong after you enter the demands of parenthood.

If you have any unresolved issues within your relationship it's best they are addressed before this section is discussed with your adoption assessor. Due to the nature and detail of questions in this category, pre-existing relationship issues may surface and the homestudy will not go forward until the assessor believes you are committed to resolving them.

For example, during the relationship discussion with the assessor it is discovered that the wife has lingering feelings of resent and hostility toward her husband about his alcohol addiction. He has successfully completed treatment; however she is still bitter over the "lost time" in their relationship when frequenting bars was more important to her husband than spending time with her. The adoption assessor will not commence a therapy session in the middle of a homestudy interview, but he or she will ask for proof (usually counseling) that the wife's emotions are being addressed and that it will not interfere with the couple raising a child.

Religious Affiliations and/or Spiritual Beliefs:

You will be asked about your religious and/or spiritual beliefs. For the sake of this book religion is defined as a divinely inspired fundamental set of beliefs and practices generally agreed upon by a number of persons or sects - often containing a moral code governing the conduct of life and human affairs. E.g. Judaism, Christianity and Islam. Spirituality is defined as the state or quality of being dedicated to

God, spiritual things, or values, especially as contrasted with material or temporal ones.

Religion and spirituality can exist individually but are often believed in and practiced simultaneously. Be prepared to discuss what you believe in, if you believe in anything at all.

You will be asked if you subscribe to any particular religion or spirituality, if you pray, what prayer means in your life and how it relates to your relationship with God. You will be asked if you attend religion or spiritual services and if you participate in any traditional or non-traditional religious or spiritual ceremonies. Depending on what you believe (or don't) you may or may not be offended by this question. The best advice I have is to be yourself and do not all of a sudden become "religious or spiritual" just for the sake of the homestudy, as your assessor is likely to see through this. There are birthparents who want their child to grow up in a home that consistently attends religious services, some that don't care if the family believes in religion and everything in between.

Some adoptive applicants make efforts to appear more religious than they actually are. They do this because they want to appeal to stakeholders and they don't want a lack of religious beliefs to count against them. There may be an adoptive couple that has been to church 3 times in their entire adult lives (for 2 weddings and 1 funeral) however in an attempt to appear more religious to a birthparent they will state during the homestudy that they are frequent church goers.

Other times adoptive applicants do attend religious services on a frequent basis, but are hesitant to discuss how involved they are in their religion or spiritual beliefs for fear that they may seem too religious. I have heard arguments for and against portraying yourself in a different religious light than you truly are.

The verdict is that you should be completely honest about where you stand on religion and spirituality. It is only fair to the birthparents that you are honest, as religion/spiritual affiliation is often important and non-negotiable to them.

Children Residing In The Home:

Minor children who live in your home and can comprehend the topic of "adoption" will be interviewed as part of the homestudy process. Your child will be asked about their school, grades, favorite subjects, involvement in sports, plans when they grow up, etc. While their interview is not as intense as yours, they will be asked how they feel about another child coming into the home, sharing their toys, sharing their parents, and the role they will play in the child's life. It's normal for children to go through age appropriate adjustment behaviors when major changes take place in the home. However your assessor will be looking for any sings that your current child may have significant difficulty adjusting, or that they may cause significant adjustment problems in the adopted child.

I once asked an 11 year old biological child about how he was going to treat his newly adopted sibling. He responded with "I'm going to tell them what to do, you know, show them how we do things around here." On the surface this statement sounds okay. You think, "Oh how nice, this child is going to be very helpful to the adopted child." However I've been doing this long enough to know that you cannot take things at face value.

After exploring the comment further I learned that this biological child had intentions on "bossing" around the adopted child and making them do all of his chores. I also learned that this child was not happy about the adoption and did not want any siblings at all. While this situation did not disqualify the applicants from adopting, I had to inform the parents of their child's inner turmoil so that it could be addressed. I had a frank discussion with the adoptive applicants and the biological child so that the biological child could learn more positive, encouraging and welcoming ways to interact with an incoming adopted child.

It is in your best interest to prepare your biological children for their interview but do not "tell" them what to say. Adoption assessors are trained to know when a child has been "groomed" to give certain responses. If your assessor suspects that you have "groomed" your child to supply robotic type responses, your assessor may question your integrity and comment about it in the "additional assessor observations" section. The best thing you can do is to discuss with your child why it's necessary for them to be interviewed, and encourage them to remain calm and to be on their best behavior! Do not put pressure on them by saying things such as "this is a big interview for mommy and daddy and your answers could make or break us." Number one that is entirely too much pressure on a child and it will make them nervous. Number two, it's likely not true, as most homestudy approvals and denials are not contingent upon biological child interviews, unless a "disqualifying reason" is discovered during such interview, which is rare.

Absent or Part-Time Children:

Absent or part –time children refer to children who are permanent members of the home but do not spend the night in the home often, and children who only visit the home on a part-time basis. In any case the adoption assessor will be talking to this person in order to assess their relationship with the adoptive applicants and how they feel about adopted children coming into the home. If the absent or part-time child has great things to say about being in your home then this part will be simple. However if their comments are less than stellar, this could cause some problems for you.

Consider the following: An adoptive father applicant has a daughter from a previous marriage who spends every other weekend in the prospective adoptive home. The daughter states to the assessor that when she visits she feels as if her father ignores her and that her step-mother does not want her there. However when the assessor talks to the father he seems to think that he and his daughter have a great relationship and that he shows her love and respect, and showers her with attention. When the assessor questioned the daughter's stepmother about the daughter being in the home, she stated that she enjoys the daughter being in the home and that she tries to show it in her behavior. There is obviously a disconnect in this situation.

It's possible that someone is lying, the family does not communicate that well, and/or they misunderstand one another greatly. Whichever the case, before the assessor can move forward with the homestudy, this situation has to be reconciled. The assessor will likely bring everyone together to discuss all of the issues in an attempt to see what is going on, what type of help and referral may be necessary, and how the situation will impact an adoptive placement. A situation like this may not prevent you from being approved to adopt, but it will be documented within the homestudy, and if not resolved, may affect your prospects of being chosen as adoptive parents.

Non-Applicant Adults In The Home:

This category is for any adult who lives in your home but is not an adoptive applicant. Although this individual will not undergo the extreme scrutiny that adoptive applicants do, they will have to complete a criminal background check, medical exam, TB test, and a brief interview with your adoption assessor about their role (if any) in the adoptive child's life. For example, if your parents live with you the assessor will want to know how they feel about you adopting, what role they will play in the child's life and how they feel about adoption overall. What they say cannot hurt your chances of being approved, unless the interview uncovers a disqualifying event that you failed to disclose on your application. If your non-applicant adult has a disqualifying event on their record, they will have to move out before you can be approved to adopt.

Attitudes And Beliefs Regarding Adoption Issues:

Children are placed for adoption due to a variety of reasons. Sometimes birthparents don't feel prepared to care for a child. Other times circumstances are not safe or healthy for the child. You will be asked your opinion about birthparents who are not able to care for their children due to the following reasons:

1. Birthparents who sexually abuse their children

2. Birthparents who physically abuse their children

3. Birthparents who abuse drugs and/or alcohol

4. Birthparents who have mental health issues

5. Birthparents who have a low IQ and cannot take care of their children

6. Birthparents who choose to not parent their child for a variety of reasons – such as wanting to pursue a career, not interested in parenting, or stating that they don't have the time

Your assessor will also ask about your preference for an open/semi-open or closed adoption. An open adoption may include visits and/or picture exchanges between the adoptive family and birthparents, semi-open may include pictures only and closed may include no contact or pictures whatsoever. Definitions and availability of open/semi-open and closed adoptions may vary from state to state. Have a candid discussion with your adoption assessor about your options.

Narrative:

The narrative section of the homestudy includes 12 intensive questions that explore your thoughts, ideas and perceptions about a variety of issues. All of the questions during the homestudy are important, however the narrative questions make up the "heart of the homestudy." Up until this point joint applicants have been interviewed together. However for the 12 narrative questions your assessor will separate and question you individually. The purpose behind the individual interviews is to determine if the applicants are consistent with the tone of their answers. Later I'll show you the problems that occur when applicant's answers are not consistent.

Following are the 12 narrative questions asked during most homestudies. Although you may experience a variation in the questions based on the state you live in, the content is generally the same which means you'll still be ready for any question that comes your way! Although I encourage you to give original answers, I've included examples of the good -vs- the not so good answers I've seen over the years. Good answers produce better quality and more competitive homestudies. Applicants who end up with "good homestudies" are usually chosen to adopt quicker. Not so good answers equal answers that don't give enough information, are vague or don't quite touch on the topic. After reading this section you'll feel more at ease about this part of your homestudy. Let's GO!

1. *Appearance and general personality*

This one is easy. Your assessor will write a brief summary of your appearance, noting your hair color, eye color and body frame size. (Heads up: Your assessor may ask how much you weigh. If they do and you are sensitive about this or don't want it documented, simply ask if they can just document your body type i.e. small, medium, large, height/weight proportionate, etc. Most adoption assessors will gladly comply with this request.

The personality part is usually up to the assessor. They will describe your personality based on their interaction with you during the homestudy. However some assessors will ask for your input on this.

A note about personality: Personalities run the gamut. I have observed applicants who I would describe as "open, engaging, friendly, funny, and sweet." I have also observed applicants who I would describe as "closed, disengaged, disinterested, bored, indifferent, condescending, and know it alls." I totally get the whole "people are who they are and that the world should accept them" movement. However when you are applying to adopt a child you want to accentuate your more positive traits and minimize your negative ones. After all, birthparents are often looking for people they think would make "great parents" for their child.

If you happen to fall into the second category of personality descriptors, then you may want to tone it down some for the homestudy. Should you decide not to, you will annoy your assessor and in return they may not portray you as positively as you would like. You don't have to "put on" in order to receive positive remarks about your personality. Just let your positive traits shine more than your negative ones.

2. Applicant's personal history

I hope that you like talking about your immediate and extended family, because we are going to ask about them! This section is designed to gain an understanding of your upbringing, family traditions, quality of family relationships, types of discipline you received as a child, activities/sports you participated in as a child, high school activities, what you did after high school, employment history, college education, hobbies, challenges in life, successes in life, abuse/neglect in your family history, involvement with child welfare agencies, major health issues, alcohol consumption activities, drug use, and criminal history.

3. Evidence of personal and emotional maturity

Main rationale of question:
To gauge if you can realistically identify your strengths and vulnerabilities.

Good answer:
A difficult or challenging situation that you overcame and how you overcame it. For example, the pain of discovering your infertility issues, and how you overcame it and moved on to choosing adoption.

Not so good answer:
Discussing how you overcame the pain associated with having an abortion as a teenager. There is no question that this would be a difficult time in anyone's life. However no matter how you describe the

circumstances surrounding the abortion, most people have strong opinions about abortion and there is no telling how you may be perceived.

4. Describe applicant's coping skills and history of stress management

Main rationale of question:
To gauge your ability to effectively deal with stress. Considering everyone has to deal with stress of some sort, your assessor wants to know if you have a healthy and effective way of dealing with it. The adoption process can be very stressful at times and the assessor needs to know that you possess the skills to combat the associated stress.

Good answer:
Discuss healthy stress management techniques that you use. Examples include but are not limited to, exercising, talking to a trusted friend, journaling, sports, praying, deep breathing, etc.

Not so good answer:
"I don't get stressed out because I'm such a laid back person." You may believe that this is true; however the stakeholders are not likely to believe you. This means they may call your character into question, and wonder about your ability to realistically perceive and cope with stressful situations.

Some level of stress, even if it's very temporary, is a part of the human existence. So try to think of a stressful event, time, or situation in your life and how you managed it.

5. Describe applicant's stability and quality of interpersonal relationships

Main rationale of question:
To gauge the stability of relationships in your life and your ability to get along with others.

Good answer:
Discuss in detail when your current friendships began i.e. during childhood, high school or more recently. Also discuss how often you connect with your friends, and who you go to for advice. If you do not have any friends, discuss why that is and what in your life takes the place of healthy friendships.

Not so good answer:
"I don't think people need friends." "You cannot trust anyone because everyone hurts you at some point anyway."

6. Describe the level of openness each applicant has in relationships

Main rationale of question:
To gauge if you are a judgmental person.

Good answer:
Give examples of how you can appreciate individual differences in people, and how you are open to different opinions than yours.

Not so good answer:
"There is not a judgmental bone in my body." Well, you may think so but your assessor knows that the average person has had at least one judgmental thought in all of their life. These types of answers

are known as "perfection pitchers." And we all know that perfect people do not exist.

7. Describe applicant's ability to empathize with others

Main rationale of question:
To identify your ability to empathize with a birthparent who has placed their child for adoption.

Good answer:
Give an example of when you were able to empathize with someone who was dealing with a difficult situation. Discuss how this relates to being empathetic toward a birthparent that has made the selfless and difficult decision to place their child for adoption. If you struggle to feel empathy toward others that does not make you a bad person. Go ahead and state that you struggle with empathy some, but cite what measures you are taking to improve your ability to empathize.

Not so good answer:
"I don't see why the birthparent would worry about their child after giving them up." "You gave the child to capable people and that should make you feel better about the situation." Answers of this nature do not reflect any empathy toward a grieving birthparent.

8. Motivation to adopt

Maine rationale of question:
To identify if your motivation to adopt is healthy and if you have dealt with the emotions associated with infertility.

Good answer:
Give examples of why you choose adoption to grow your family.

If you have infertility issues (not all people who adopt do) discuss how you have dealt with your infertility issues. Talk about the activities you look forward to participating in with your baby. Discuss family traditions that you will include your baby in.

Not so good answer:
"This is our only option for having a family." In reality it may be, however statements like this give the impression that you prefer biological children but are "settling" for adoption. Birthparents want to know that their baby is not being adopted because it's a last resort option for a childless couple - even if it is.

9. Understanding of entitlement issues

Main rationale of question:
To identify your ability to internalize your "rights" and "responsibilities" as an adoptive parent.

Good answer:
Give examples of how you are committed to taking on full responsibility for your adopted child's well being. Emphasize that you would treat your adopted child the same way you would treat a biological child.

Not so good answer: Any answer where you hold a biological child in higher esteem than an adopted child. If you struggle with the idea of an adoptive child having the same rights and responsibilities as a biological child, you should seek counseling and/or a trusted friend to work through those feelings. Adopted children should absolutely have the same rights as biological children.

10. Ability to make and honor commitments

Main rationale of question:
To identify your ability to meet the long term needs of a child, as evidenced by your ability or inability to maintain long term relationships, and to keep promises and commitments even when it's inconvenient or difficult for you.

Good answer:
Give examples of significant long term commitments that you are fulfilling or have fulfilled. Link that to how you possess the fortitude to care for an adoptive child on a long term basis.

Not so good answer:
"I can't think of any long term commitments in my life." "I'm just not good with sticking to things." Perhaps you aren't good with crossing the finish line in life. However this is not the time to admit so.

11. Parenting skills and abilities

Main rationale for question:
To identify your ability to meet the physical, emotional and psychological needs of a child.

Good answer:
Describe the nature and extent of prior childcare experience. This could be but is not limited to babysitting, interacting with the children of friends/relatives, church daycare, summer camps, etc. Discuss your ability to read non-verbal cues from children and the types of discipline you would use to correct behaviors (do not mention spanking.) Even if you believe in spanking, stakeholders may not and some may even have strong opinions against it. There are plenty of

effective non-physical disciplinary methods available to you. If necessary your assessor can help you think of some. If you do not have any experience with being around children, focus on your best ideas for raising a child.

Not so good answer:
"I don't know anything about kids." You might not, but this does not make you look attractive to a birthparent that is looking for someone to adopt their child. If you truly don't know anything about children you can state something along the lines of "While my exposure to children has not been as much as I would like, I'm currently doing some things to improve my parenting skills such as, reading parenting books/magazines, volunteering in a facility that serves children, and talking to others who care for children about their experiences.

12. Willingness to utilize a "hands on" approach in parenting

Main rationale for question:
To identify your ability to utilize a variety of behavior management techniques.

Good answer:
Discuss your willingness to verbally instruct and "model" appropriate behaviors for your child.

Not so good answer:
"If I tell my child how to do something they should get it." "I should not have to show them too." Effective parenting is balanced parenting. Sometimes your child will only need verbal instructions and other times they will need you to show them how to do something.

Support System:

Do you have family and friends whom you can utilize as a support system? Your assessor will make comments about who in your life is available for support when you need it. While you may feel as if you and your partner don't need others, most people realize that no man is an island. It makes you appear stronger and more balanced if you have someone who you can turn to in life.

If you do not have any close family or friends as a support system, start to think about any neighbors, fellow community residents, church members or colleagues who you can list as a support system.

Guardianship Plan:

You will be asked who you have elected to raise your child if you and your spouse become incapacitated or die. The person or couple you choose should be someone who has the love, emotional stability and financial resources to take care of a child. Stakeholders will be reading this section and you will look more appealing if you have chosen outstanding guardians. You can change your guardianship choice at any time.

Family Strengths and Needs:

This section will address strengths and needs as identified by the assessor and the applicants. Examples of family strengths are: strong and stable marriage, stable employment, enjoys activities together, communicates well with one another, strong ties to church, and strong ties to the community. Examples of family needs are: ongoing education and training of adoption related issues as child moves through developmental stages, continued counseling to deal with unresolved fertility issues, and development of a guardianship plan if both adoptive parents were to become incapacitated or die. These are just examples and you should start thinking now about what your family's strengths and needs are.

Feel free to be open and honest about what your needs are. If you have strengths that your assessor has not identified, ask that they add this information if it will add to the quality of your homestudy.

Additional Assessor Observations:

There are situations, questions and other issues that arise during the homestudy process in which there is nowhere else to document what the assessor has witnessed. In situations like this assessors use the "additional assessor observations" section to record their concerns.

Race:

You should be open and honest about why you have chosen not to adopt a child from a particular race. A Caucasian couple indicated on their application for adoption that they would "consider" any race except African American. Their reasoning was that there were no African American children in their neighborhood, and they assumed that the child would not feel comfortable. The assessor researched the demographics of this couple's neighborhood, and discovered that there were also no Latino, Asian or Native American residents living in that area.

So what was the *true* reason this couple would not consider an African American child? Only this couple knows the answer to that. However it was not the reason that they gave, as they were willing to consider children from other races that were not represented in their neighborhood either. This sort of inconsistency is a concern and would be documented in the homestudy. You have the right to choose a child from any background that you would like. However if your reasoning for excluding a particular race is contradictory, your character will be called into question.

Skin Tone:

Some Caucasian applicants may consider Latino children but not African American children. Sometimes they make this decision because they may not be comfortable with a child who has dark skin. However keep in mind that many Latino babies may start off with lighter skin and get darker as time goes on.

What happens if you have agreed to adopt a Latino baby, but after that baby is born you discover that they baby looks more African American? Do you go through with the adoption because you made a commitment? Do you back out of the adoption after you have committed your emotions and finances? These are not easy questions to answer. This is why you really need to think about why you will not consider a particular race, and how that rationalization affects what you would do if a child in your "will consider" category is born but resembles a child in your "will not consider category."

The problem without a name:

I've come across situations where the husband applicant does not appear to be "into" the homestudy as much as the wife applicant. Neither one admitted this but it was apparent based on his demeanor and comments. Adoption assessors know when one spouse wants to adopt and the other does not. We are trained to identify subtleties and small nuances in martial relationships as it relates to the adoption process. It is vitally important that both spouses be on board with the adoption. If we suspect that one spouse is not on board, this concern will be documented in the homestudy.

Summary:

- The adoption homestudy is used as a tool to either approve or deny applicants the opportunity to adopt.
- The title and training of the person completing your homestudy will vary. Following are some examples of the titles of such person: adoption assessor, homestudy assessor, adoption case worker, adoption case manager, adoption counselor, homestudy coordinator and homestudy counselor.
- Birthparents and adoption placement workers (otherwise known as stakeholders) are the ones who choose the adoptive parents.
- Given the consequences of intentional and unintentional omission of a criminal record - it is advisable that you go to great lengths to remember, research and dig as deep as possible to recall any criminal record that you may have.
- If you are adopting a child from a different racial or cultural background you need to consider how welcoming your community will be toward them.
- You are required to document any marital relationship you've had, whether it was short lived, annulled or a nightmare!
- Be open and honest about your religious/spiritual affiliation or lack thereof. It is only fair to the birthparents as religion/spiritual affiliation is often important and non-negotiable to them.

- If your non-applicant adult household member has a disqualifying event on their record they will have to move out before you can be approved to adopt.
- Definitions and availability of open/semi-open and closed adoptions may vary from state to state. Have a candid discussion with your adoption assessor about your options.
- You will need to elect someone to raise your child if you and your spouse become incapacitated or die.
- You will need to complete a medical exam to show that you are suitable to adopt. The adoption assessor is not looking for someone in perfect health. They need to ensure that the adoptive applicant does not have any medical conditions that would prevent them from properly caring for a child.
- You should pick someone who can write a positive and well balanced reference on your behalf. Avoid references that are over the top or lackluster.

Insider Tips:

- It's important to provide your adoption assessor with quality information so that they can write a homestudy that "sells" you to stakeholders and sets you apart from your competitors.
- If you are sure of the age of the child you want to adopt, you can appear proactive and impressive by purchasing a car seat before adopting the child.

- If you are currently in the military that may concern some birthparents, as they may wonder if you will be around to care for the child. Be sure to have your adoption assessor discuss how you plan on making room in your schedule to care for a child even if you have a busy schedule (especially travel) due to military obligations.
- If your neighborhood has great crime statistics ask your adoption assessor to highlight that in your homestudy. This will make your homestudy sound more impressive.
- Excited about the prospects of adopting a child from a different racial background? Have your assessor document the things you are willing to do to make the child feel welcomed into your life. Examples include but are not limited to, educating yourself on their culture, making new friends from that culture or moving your residence.
- If your school district is rated excellent or excellent with distinction, mention this so that your adoption professional can highlight it in the homestudy.
- Ensure that your adoption assessor writes a narrative either accentuating your stable residential history, or minimizing the impact of your frequent address changes by highlighting positive reasons for the movement.
- If you've made frequent job changes you will want to minimize the impact of appearing unstable. Ask your assessor to acknowledge this fact in the homestudy. Then pivot away from the issue and state something along the lines of, "I realize that I've held 6 jobs over the last 6 years." "I was undergoing transition in my life and it took awhile for me to find a career that best suited me." "While I understand someone may question my ability to be a stable parent, rest assured that my

frequent job changes are in no way indicative of my ability to provide a stable environment for a child, as evidenced by the number of years I've babysat nieces, nephews, etc or volunteered in the church nursery, community center, etc." "I am now confident that I have found a career path that I can build on while continuing to provide a loving and stable home for a child."

- Single applicants should still be encouraged about the homestudy and adoption process. Birthparents do choose single parents to adopt their children. However as a single person be careful how you address your relationship status. If you are single and not involved with anyone then simply state that. However you will need to mention the role any suitor who comes into your life would play in your child's life. Birthparents need to know that you will remain committed to raising your adopted child, even after you meet Mr. or Mrs. Wonderful.

- If you have any unresolved issues within your relationship, it's best to address them before starting the homestudy process. Due to the nature and detail of homestudy questions, pre-existing relationship issues may surface during the interview. If this occurs, the homestudy will not go forward until the assessor believes you are committed to resolving your issues.

- If your assessor discovers contradictory information when interviewing non-applicant household members this could be problematic for the applicants. Before moving forward with the homestudy, the contradiction has to be reconciled. The assessor will likely bring everyone together to discuss all of the issues in an attempt to see

what is going on, what type of help and referral may be necessary, and how the situation will impact an adoptive placement. While a situation of this nature may not prevent you from being approved to adopt, it will be documented within the homestudy, and if not resolved, may affect your prospects of being chosen by a stakeholder.
- If you have an unflattering personality and refuse to tone it down for the homestudy, you will annoy your assessor and in return they may not portray you as positively as you would like in your homestudy.

Red Flags:

Infertility Issues

- Adoption assessors are keenly aware of the impact that infertility has on a marriage. A red flag goes up in the assessor's mind if a couple asserts that infertility has had no effect on their marriage whatsoever.

Religion

- Depending on what you believe (or don't) you may or may not be offended by questions on this topic. The best thing you can do is to be yourself, and not suddenly become "religious or spiritual" for the sake of the homestudy, as your assessor is likely to see through this.

Biological Children Interviews

- Adoption assessors are trained to know when a child has been "groomed" to recite certain responses. If your assessor suspects that you have "groomed" your child to supply robotic type responses, your assessor may question your integrity and comment about this in the "additional assessor observations" section.

Applicant Motivation

Adoption assessors can detect when one spouse wants the adoption to occur and the other does not. We are trained to pick up on subtleties and small nuances in martial relationships as it relates to the adoption process. Ensure that you are both on the same page about adopting before embarking on this journey.

3 ALL INTERVIEWS ARE NOT CREATED EQUAL

The appointment you must be prepared for

After your adoption application has been reviewed, you will be contacted by an adoption assessor to schedule your first homestudy appointment. Individual states vary regarding the number of visits required to complete the homestudy. In the state of Ohio the assessor is required to make at least one face to face visit. However given the time that it takes to complete an adoptive homestudy, more than 1 visit will be necessary. In most cases it will take 3 visits, each lasting 2-3 hours, to complete this process.

The style of the homestudy interview and the time between each visit will vary based on adoption assessor style and preference. In some instances phone or video chat visits will be acceptable. In other instances each visit will occur in person, with some being in your home and others in a public setting. Don't be afraid to discuss appointment options with your assessor. Often times adoptive families erroneously think that speaking up will affect their chances of adopting.

A word of caution: Try not to be overly rigid or dominate the appointment setting process. For example, an adoptive applicant who will only meet on Monday mornings between 8-11 am is not being very accommodating. This does not give your adoption assessor much flexibility in setting appointments with you. They may also question your ability to be "flexible with child rearing" – something that they associate with effective parenting. You may also get labeled as "inflexible" somewhere in your homestudy. This is something that you want to avoid considering stakeholders could see this.

Following is an example of the "typical" interview process:

First Visit:

The adoption assessor will discuss the homestudy process with you. This is the time for you to ask any questions that you may have. I have found that most adoptive parents – although bursting with questions in their heads – tend to shy away from asking questions at the first visit. Perhaps they do not have any questions at this point, but most often their lack of questions is due to nervousness and the perceived power they believe the adoption assessor has over them. While this is true to a certain extent, we have more to gain by approving than denying you. We want to approve you because we love building families, but we also stand to gain a significant profit if the adoption finalizes. Once you realize that we operate from this mindset, you'll feel less intimidated and anxious about asking questions.

The assessor will start the homestudy by asking specific questions to assess your appropriateness and readiness to adopt. (The various questions required for the homestudy are covered in Chapter 2.)

This is not about being the perfect couple (or single person.) This is about determining if you possess the appropriate communication, parenting, life and stress management skills to effectively parent a child. At the conclusion of the first visit, you will discuss when and where to conduct your next visit.

Second Visit:

This visit is a continuation of the first visit. However just when you think that this interview will continue in the same manner as the first – there will be a surprise! This time the adoption assessor will separate and interview the applicants individually. The purpose of separate interviews is to ensure that both applicants are on the same page about adopting. While applicants are not expected to give identical answers, it is expected that the "tone" and "feel" of your answers will be in sync.

Consider The Following Responses To The Question: *Why have you decided to adopt?*

RESPONSES THAT ARE IN SYNC

Wife:

"Long before we even knew about our fertility issues, we talked about adopting a child.
I think that adoption is a great way for us to build our family."

Husband:

"We've always talked about how we want lots of little feet running around our home. We were fine with either biological or adopted children. Once we learned of our fertility issues we knew that adoption was the way to go. It's really a lifelong dream and I would love to see it come true."

What It All Means:

Although the applicants did not give identical answers, they gave answers that were "in sync" or "in agreement" with their motivation to adopt.

RESPONSES THAT ARE IN SYNC– BUT THAT CONTAIN SLIGHT DIFFERENCES OF OPINION

Wife:

"We are having fertility issues. We would love to have biological children, but it's just not happening for us at the moment. It's very difficult to accept that I cannot have biological children. I cry daily because I really want to be a mom and it's unfair that it hasn't happened for me. However, we do see adoption as an opportunity to still build a family."

Husband:

"We are having problems having our own kids. We would prefer to have biological children, you know, little people that act and look like us – but I guess it's just not meant to happen that way. I feel bad about our situation at times, but I realize that it's not the worst thing that could happen in life. Considering we have decided to move forward with adoption, we hardly think about our fertility problems anymore."

What It All Means:

The applicant responses vary slightly on how the infertility is impacting them, yet they are both adopting for the same reason. Although the adoption assessor will encourage this couple to resolve their fertility issues, the answers they gave are not likely to stall the progress of the homestudy.

RESPONSES THAT ARE OUT OF SYNC AND CONTAIN EXTREME INCONSISTENCIES

Wife:

"We have been trying to have a baby for the last 5 years and it just hasn't happened for us. I'm devastated and I don't think I'll ever get over not being able to have my own children. It's extremely frustrating to have spent over $20,000 on fertility treatments and to not have a baby to show for it. Basically I see adoption as my only option."

Husband:

"There's really no specific reason. It's just something that has always been on my heart. I've always wanted to be a dad and rather than waiting to have our own children, I thought that adoption would be the quickest path to parenthood."

What It All Means:

In this instance the applicants gave extremely different reasons for wanting to adopt. The adoption assessor would not be able to finish the homestudy interview until this inconsistency was resolved. A very candid discussion would need to occur about why they supplied significantly different answers. The couple would probably require counseling before they would be ready to adopt. The adoption assessor may also leave comments in the homestudy about what was said during their separate interviews.

Advice: Before you start the homestudy interview process talk with your co-applicant to ensure that you are on the same page (not necessarily identical) as it pertains to your motivation to adopt. If you have any unresolved issues about your fertility or other adoption related issues, ensure that you have a plan to work through and resolve them before starting your homestudy.

Third and Subsequent Visits:

Your assessor will answer any questions that you have and complete a safety audit. The safety audit is not a white glove inspection of your home. It's a walkthrough of your home to ensure it is a safe place for a child to live. (For a full description of the safety audit – see Chapter 4.) Your assessor will also review some of the paperwork you were assigned previously for completeness. Lastly, you will receive information on the next step in the homestudy process. Depending on the agency you are working with, the assessor may allow you to review your completed homestudy before it's finalized. You will be asked to inform your assessor of any needed corrections as they pertain to name spellings, dates or facts. Sometimes applicants request grammar or content corrections. If you have a serious concern about the subjective content, then discuss it with your assessor to see if this is something they are willing to change. However it's their decision whether they will make these changes or not.

Remember that this is someone else's assessment, and they may not take kindly to your suggestions to rearrange it. In fact, your assessor may take offense to your suggestions to change the subjective content portion of their assessment.

Summary:

- States vary regarding the number of visits required but you will have at least one face to face visit in your home.
- In addition to visits being held in your home, some of your visits may occur in public or while utilizing certain types of technology such as video chatting.
- The homestudy is not about being perfect, rather your assessor wants to ensure that you possess the necessary communication, parenting, life and stress management skills to care for a child.
- After reviewing your homestudy, it's best to stick to informing your assessor about objective and factual errors only.

Insider Tips:

- Don't be afraid to discuss appointment options with your assessor. Often times adoptive families erroneously think that speaking up will affect their chances to adopt.
- If you are overly rigid in setting your homestudy appointments, your assessor may also question your ability to be "flexible with child rearing" – something that is associated with effective parenting.
- Don't be afraid to ask questions during your homestudy interviews. Most assessors desire to approve you because in addition to wanting to find homes for children, they stand to gain a substantial profit if your adoption finalizes.
- While the first interview will likely be a joint applicant interview, the applicants will be separated (usually without prior warning) at a subsequent appointment to assess if they are "on the same page" about adopting.

Red Flags:

- If joint applicants have significantly different reasons for adopting, especially if those reasons are indicative of unresolved marital or infertility issues, these issues will need to be resolved before the assessor will continue with the homestudy.

4 THE PAPER TRAIL

Breeze through the additional paperwork associated with the homestudy

In addition to the interviews there are additional documents that need to be completed as part of your homestudy. You will complete some of the paperwork, and some of it will be completed by other entities. Following is a list of your required paperwork.

Paperwork Completed By The Applicant(s):

Application For Child Placement

Remember to be as accurate as possible when filling out your initial application to adopt. Intentionally falsifying information is grounds for declining your application. If you are unsure of some of the answers, research them until you are certain. Sometimes applicants will *simply* go to another agency if they were denied by the first one. It is possible that the new agency you approach will find out that you were denied by the first agency. Therefore it's best to be totally and completely honest during the application phase.

Financial Statement

It's a common misconception that one must be wealthy in order to adopt. This is simply not true as I have approved adoptive applicants from a variety of income brackets. You will be required to fill out a financial statement that documents your income, expenses, assets and liabilities. Your assessor will review the financial statement for completeness. It really doesn't matter how much money you make. I know that's hard to believe, but it's true. We just need to know that you earn enough to support an additional person. How then do we determine this? It's simple. The rule we follow is more income than expenses. If you can show that you bring in more than you spend, we will conclude that you can afford to take care of a child. If you have more expenses than income, find a way to reduce your expenses or increase your income so that your assessor will feel comfortable with your financial situation, and will have no reason to document concerns about your ability to financially provide for a child. If a stakeholder discovers that there is a question about your ability to financially provide for a child, this will decrease your chances of being chosen as an adoptive parent.

In addition to proving that you can afford to take care of a child, it is equally important that your financial statement make sense. Red flags go up if your documented income doesn't match your overall financial picture.

For example if a married couple documents on their financial statement that they earn $20,000 a month after taxes, have $5000 in monthly living expenses, but only have $2000 in savings, the assessor is going to wonder where the rest of their money is. It doesn't matter what they do with their disposable income, it just needs to be accounted for. Finance is always a red flag area for adoption assessors because applicants like to over inflate their financial situation. They manipulate numbers to portray that they have more assets and income and/or less debt than they actually have. Sometimes they attempt to make seasonal income (such as bonuses and contract jobs) look like steady income – when it's usually not. Please be mindful that your assessor will be looking for these types of entries on your financial statement.

Be prepared to verify your income with an employer letter, paycheck stubs, W-2, or income tax forms. You may also need to show information on your savings, insurance coverage, investments, debts, and credit report.

Child Characteristics Checklist

You will review and identify a list of various social, emotional, psychological, learning and medical conditions that may or may not exist in a child. You will need to identify what you will and will not consider when adopting a child. If you check that you will not consider a specific condition, you will not be considered for a child who has that condition – even if it's only a mild form. Thus it is sometimes best to chose "will consider", get the facts of the referral and make your decision based on the facts. In some states, "not applicable" is not a choice on this form so you must choose either "will consider" or "will not consider". Try to fill this form out accurately the first time, as your agency may charge you for an amendment if you change your preferences after your homestudy has been finalized. Of course it's understandable if you change your preferences after completing your trainings and learning about different conditions.

MEPA Form

In short the Multi Ethnic Placement Act prohibits adoption professionals from considering race as a factor when placing children. Your agency will require that you sign a form indicating that you have read about and understand this act.

Trainings

Most states require specific trainings as part of the adoptive homestudy process. Your agency may also require additional trainings that are not necessarily mandated by your state.

Training requirements vary by state but have similar characteristics. You will likely be required to complete at least 36 hours of some sort of book or live training. Your adoption agency will usually provide you with the material or a link, and you will write brief paragraphs about what you learned. Each applicant must do their own homework. Try not to look at one another's answers because the training is for your benefit and everyone gets something different out of it. Even if you already have children or you think that you already "know" about the topics, you will still learn something new and should approach the training with an open mind. If you are adopting a child from a different race or culture, pay special attention to cross cultural issues. You may think that cross cultural issues are common sense - and some of it is – but there's a lot to be learned that will benefit you and your adopted child.

Autobiographies

Be prepared to write your life story! It doesn't have to be a novel but you will be asked to write about how you grew up, your family, your education, and major events in your life. Depending on your agency you may be provided with a template to follow, or you may have to start it from scratch. Either way, there is no right or wrong answer, just be open and have fun talking about yourself!

Household Evacuation Maps

During the safety audit your assessor will check to ensure that you have an evacuation map posted in your basement and on every floor in your home. You will also need to list where your family is to meet in the event of an emergency – such as the basement or on the front tree lawn. We understand that you are already familiar with the layout of your home. However, for liability reasons this is our way of documenting that you have an escape plan in place to ensure your child's safety. As your adopted child ages it will be beneficial for them to know how to get out of the house if there were an emergency. It is also helpful for babysitters, extended family members and others who may be responsible for the care of your child during an emergency.

The map must include a drawing of each room, along with primary and alternate escape routes. Many times the primary escape route is a door and the alternate escape route is a window. If a room does not have an alternate escape route, then you should document that on your map. At times applicants hang up extremely elaborate and technical maps, which are too difficult for the average person to understand at first glance. Your evacuation map should serve as a quick visual aide that gives instructions on how to exit your home during an emergency. Your map should be simple yet effective. Your assessor should be able to glance at your evacuation map and immediately know how to escape from each room in your home. If your map is too technical and cumbersome to understand, your assessor may ask you to re-do it before they will approve it. Most times when people re-do their evacuation maps we have to sit there and wait for them to finish. When this occurs applicants tend to feel intimidated and rushed while they are attempting to correct and simplify their maps. This is never a comfortable situation for anyone. Although we love working with applicants, we do want to get out of your home and back to our own families as quickly as possible. Therefore it is beneficial to everyone that the evacuation maps are done correctly the first time.

Emergency Phone Numbers

States vary but in general you will have to list the following numbers in an easy to find place (usually the refrigerator): the fire department, non-emergency police, ambulance, poison control, recommending agency and placing agency.

Marriage License

Some people are legally married but do not have a marriage license. Some religions do not believe in marriage being authenticated by the court system. However they are "legally" married through their local clergy. As long as the marriage is documented on paper it is generally accepted as legal proof of marriage. If this is a concern for you, check with your agency to see what type of documentation they are willing to accept.

Signed Copy Of Divorce Decree

If you have been married before your assessor will want to verify that the marriage has been legally terminated.

Copy Of Recent Pet Vaccination Records

Your veterinarian will need to indicate in a letter that your animals are not vicious and will not be harmful toward children.

Copy Of Driver's License

This is requested to verify identification.

Copy Of Auto Insurance

Assessors have to verify that adopted children will be transported in automobiles that are adequately insured. You will need to carry at least your state's minimum coverage.

Copy Of Health Insurance

You will need to show that you can provide for your child's medical needs.

Copy Of Adoption Decree For Each Previously Adopted Child

If you have adopted before, your assessor will want to verify this.

Copy Of Military Discharge

If you have a less than honorable military discharge, you will need to explain the reasoning to your assessor. They may request additional information depending on the circumstances. I.e. if you were discharged for medical or mental health reasons, you may need a statement from a medical provider that indicates this is no longer an issue, and that you are suitable to adopt.

Paperwork Completed By Other Entities On Behalf Of The Applicant(s):

Copy Of Previous Homestudy

If another agency has completed a homestudy on your behalf, your current assessor will want to review it to ensure that you were not turned down to adopt, and to see if there are any red flags to be aware of.

Letter Of Reference From Previous Homestudy Agency

Your current agency will ask your previous agency for a reference regarding your suitability to adopt. If you did not leave your previous agency on good terms, it's advisable that you explain the situation to your current assessor so that there will not be any surprises later on in the homestudy process.

BCI And FBI Fingerprinting

Instead of calling and/or driving all around town to find out where to get prints done, try your local Division of Motor Vehicles. They do it electronically and will have you in and out in no time. Their results also seem to come back quicker than specialty fingerprinting companies.

If you have not lived in your state within the last 5 years, you may have to obtain a background check from your previous state of residence. Your agency will provide you with more information on this.

Child Abuse Check

This check will determine if you have ever been convicted of a crime against a minor. If your results are positive for harming a child in any way, you will not be approved to adopt.

Safety Audit

Contrary to popular belief this is not a white glove inspection. It's an overall inspection of the safety of your home. The adoptive home must be clear of clutter on the stairs, in walkways or anywhere else a safety hazard could exist. All medicines must be locked up or kept out of a child's reach. Firearms and other weapons must be locked up and the ammunition must be kept separately. If you have anything other than city water you will need to have your water tested and approved as a safe supply, or you must agree to purchase a continuous supply of purified water for the entire home – not just for cooking. Emergency phone numbers need to be posted in an easy to spot area in your kitchen. All doors that lock must open from either side, you must have a working toilet in the home, working smoke alarm, UL approved fire extinguisher, UL approved kerosene heater, and written evacuation plan on each level of the home that contains a primary and alternate escape route. Cribs, bassinets and child car seats can be obtained after you adopt, but you must verbally or in writing agree to purchase them once a child has been placed with you.

Fire Inspection

You will need to contact your local fire department to have this form completed. This inspection ensures that your home does not contain any fire hazards. If it does you will need to have any and all fire hazards fixed before your homestudy can be approved. The fire department may charge you a small fee to complete this inspection.

Psychological Evaluation

There are three instances in which a psychological evaluation will be required as part of your homestudy. The first is if your state requires it for all applicants. The second is if your agency requires one for all applicants, regardless if your state does or not. The third reason is if your behavior and/or comments suggest that you have an untreated mental health condition. In this instance your agency/assessor will ask you to submit to a psychological exam to ensure that you are an appropriate candidate to adopt.

So, how can you avoid being asked to submit to a psychological? Act normal! Seriously, most times a psychological is not necessary. However, if your assessor suspects a problem they will definitely ask you to complete one.

Medical Evaluation

You will need to explain any current health problems and undergo a physical exam by a licensed medical provider. Individual states will vary in regard to what type of medical provider is acceptable to complete the exam. The adoption assessor is not looking for someone in perfect health. They need to ensure that the adoptive applicant does not have any medical conditions that would prevent them from properly caring for a child. You could have every medical condition under the sun, but if none of your conditions prevent you from being able to parent a child then your physical health will not be an issue.

I once had an applicant avoid all forms of stress, and listen to light jazz for several days leading up to her medical exam. She wanted to guarantee that her already "good" blood pressure numbers came back even more impressive. While this is admirable it was not necessary.

Your medical provider will need to specifically comment on your ability to become an adoptive parent. Adoption agencies often receive medical forms where the doctor has only commented on the applicant's health status – but they do not mention anything about their suitability to adopt. If this happens to you, you will have to take the form back to your medical provider's office to obtain the adoption suitability comments. If your medical provider indicates that you are not suitable to adopt from a medical prospective, then you may not get approved to adopt. This normally only happens if you are severely debilitated by a physical or mental health condition. If this occurs, you could ask your doctor if there is anything that you could do to become medically suitable to adopt. If you do not like the answer given to you, you are always welcome to obtain a second opinion.

References:

References are required by all states and give insight into your suitability to adopt. You will be asked to supply the names, addresses and phone numbers of 3-4 non-relative references. The references should be very familiar with you and have seen you respond to a variety of life situations. If you have worked with children in a professional capacity you will be asked to supply a reference from someone who has observed your work with children.

Reference questions vary based on the form that your agency uses, however all references typically contain the following pieces of information: name, address, phone number, how long the reference has known the applicant, in what capacity they know you, their opinion about your suitability to adopt, how a child would be treated in your home, your relationship with other relatives, the quality of your marriage or other significant relationships, your personality traits, and any reason they feel you should not adopt. Whew! Do you see why you must be _absolutely careful_ when choosing references?

Here is the advice I have for you when it comes to choosing references. Pick someone who will without a doubt write a glowing reference about you. (Comments that your references make are included in the homestudy, thus stakeholders will see them). This may seem like common sense but there have been issues in the past with assessors receiving references that have outright stated that an applicant "is not prepared to parent" and that "they should not be allowed to adopt." This is not something that you want to go into your homestudy.

Let's say that you have a reference in mind, but you're unsure as to what they might say about you. Make this really easy on yourself and do not use them! Period! The stakes are entirely too high to gamble with your references. You might be thinking "but this person is one of my only few choices." I can understand that, but you are going to have to look long and hard for someone else. Your adoption is too important to risk receiving a questionable reference.

References usually fall into four categories

1. **The lackluster reference :**

"I have known Mrs. X for 5 days. Mrs. X is a nice person and she likes kids. I suppose that she will take good care of a child."

2. **The well balanced reference:**

"I have known Mrs. X for 1 year. I have seen her interact with children at the community center, and I notice that the children are very receptive toward her. When a child is in need of something she will stop whatever she is doing to attend to that child. Mrs. X and her husband appear to have a happy marriage. It seems as if Mrs. X loves children, has a kind heart and would make a great adoptive parent."

3. **The over the top reference:**

"I have known Mrs. X for 1 year. And I can honestly say that she the most beautiful, uncompromising, and perfect soul that the human race has ever seen. She is flawless beyond measure and I have never known her to do any wrong, tell a lie, or even have a bad day. She constantly smiles, laughs and is always in a chipper mood. Mrs. X is an absolute saint and I cannot think of anyone else who would make a better parent than she would."

Okay so this example is a little extreme, but you get my drift. The tone of this example is what I need you to pay attention to. It's too over the top and in the minds of most readers, it's not believable. You don't have to be perfect to be chosen as an adoptive parent. You need to be a well balanced and normal human being.

4. The problem reference:

"I have known Mrs. X for 1 year. We became acquainted after volunteering together at Summer Youth Camp. I do not think she is appropriate to become an adoptive parent. She is mean, self centered and extremely impatient. Anytime one of the kids would ask for a snack she would become irritated and tell the child to ask someone else to help them because she was busy (she was usually texting on her cell phone when she claimed to be "busy.") I refuse to recommend Mrs. X to adopt because she is not ready. She couldn't even handle the kids at camp, and one has to wonder how she got the job considering that there is a child endangerment charge on her criminal record."

The comments made prior to mentioning the child endangerment charge were definitely negative and the assessor would have to question the applicant about their legitimacy. However if the child endangerment charge was found to be accurate, the homestudy process would be over and the applicant would be denied the opportunity to adopt.

You want the tone of your references to be more like example #2. Although you should not tell your references what to write, you are now prepared to guide them in regard to what makes a reference creditable, helpful and outstanding!

Summary:

- Your financial statement should show that you have more income than expenses. This will assure your assessor that you can financially support a child.
- If you indicate that you will not consider a specific characteristic/condition, you will not be considered for a child who has that condition, even if it's a mild form.
- At least 36 hours of training on adoption related issues will be required. Some agencies will give you readings and you will train yourself. Other agencies may conduct the trainings in person. If your schedule doesn't allow for in person trainings, ask if you could do it on your own.
- Because some religions do not believe that the courts should validate marriage, some couples do not have marriage licenses, but instead have validation of marriage through their local clergy. Check with your agency to see if this acceptable.
- Your veterinarian will need to provide a letter indicating that your pets will not act aggressively toward children.
- Be prepared to discuss any "less than honorable" discharges from the military.
- If you have a completed homestudy from another agency, your current agency will ask for a reference and a copy of that homestudy, to identify any red flags.
- You will need to be in contact with your local fire department to have a fire inspection of your home completed. There may be a small fee associated with this inspection.
- Your adoption assessor can request that you complete a psychological evaluation if they believe it is warranted.

- You will undergo a medical examination to ensure that you do not have any medical conditions that would prevent you from properly caring for a child.
- Make wise choices when deciding who will write your references. Properly written references can give an applicant's homestudy a great boost. Poorly written references can be very problematic.

<u>Insider Tips:</u>

- References are tricky in that if you get a negative review your assessor may question they type of parent you will be. If you get an over the top "gushing" and "oozing from the sides" reference, your assessor is likely to suspect embellishment. Applicants are required to supply 3-4 references. When assessors comment about your references in the homestudy, we only include 1-2 sentences from each reference - not the entire reference. If a part of your reference is over the top, we won't believe that part. And we do not include reference comments that we don't believe in the homestudy. This may be detrimental to you if you coached your references to make the over the top statements, in hopes that the statements would grace your homestudy. So, when asking someone to write a reference on your behalf, remind them to keep the reference positive and glowing, yet well balanced and believable.
- Under which circumstances could a reference prevent someone from adopting? If they expose a disqualifying and verifiable offense. (See Chapter 5 for disqualifying offenses.) If this occurs your assessor will research the

issue and decide if they can approve you to adopt, or if they have to deny your application. If you receive a reference that is negative, but it does not disclose a disqualifying offense, your assessor will talk to you about the concern, and ask you to correct the issue and/or find a different reference altogether. Some agencies will not tell you which one of your references provided negative feedback.

- Some agencies will charge you an "amendment fee" if you change any of your demographic preferences (age range, gender, race, etc) after your homestudy has been finalized. Therefore it's best to be sure of your preference choices before your homestudy is complete.
- You will be asked to write an autobiography. Some applicants find the process of writing about themselves quite daunting. If your agency doesn't provide you with a template to use as a guideline, there is no harm in asking for one. If your agency does not supply templates and you have to write your autobiography from scratch, ask if you are able to see an example of one.
- During the safety audit your assessor will check to ensure that you have an evacuation map posted in your basement and on every floor in your home .Your assessor should be able to glance at your evacuation map and immediately know how to escape from each room in your home. If your map is too technical and cumbersome to understand, your assessor may ask you to re-do it before they will approve it.
- If you left another adoption agency on bad terms, make sure you discuss the situation with your current assessor so that there are no surprises later on during the homestudy process.

- Going to the Division of Motor Vehicles to obtain fingerprints is typically a much faster process than getting them done at a fingerprinting specialty company.

<u>Red Flags</u>

- Make sure that your financial statement adds up. It raises a red flag if you earn $20,000 a month after taxes, have $5000 in monthly living expenses, but only have $2000 in savings. The assessor is going to question where the rest of your money is going. It doesn't matter what you do with your disposable income, it just needs to be accounted for.
- Assessors are aware of applicant's attempts to camouflage debt or over inflate income and assets.

5 APPROVED TO ADOPT! OR NOT

"Problem Approvals" and the most common reasons applicants are disqualified from adopting

At the conclusion of your homestudy, your assessor will make one of the (3) following decisions:

1. Approve and recommend the applicant(s) as adoptive parents. (This is the one you want.)

2. Approve the applicant(s) as adoptive parent(s) only.
The reason you would get this type of approval and not #1 is because the assessor has some concern regarding your ability to parent. However, the concern does not rise to the level of disqualification

Therefore the assessor is more comfortable with just "approving" you and not "approving and recommending" you. This is a nuance that most applicants and stakeholders don't pick up on anyway. However if you see this type of approval on your homestudy, feel free to ask why you did not get the "preferred" type of approval from #1 above.

3. Deny the adoption application.
If you are denied, talk to you assessor/agency to see what, if any, appeal rights you may have.

Approval

Congratulations, you have been approved to adopt! Welcome to the world of all of the other successful hoop jumpers! Once you have been approved you will receive a copy of your finalized hometstudy. You may continue to work with the agency that completed your homestudy for placement (if they offer placement services) or you may hire another agency to work with. Keep in mind that your homestudy agency may charge you a fee to transfer your homestudy. However once you have an approved homestudy you can almost always transfer it and work with any agency. There are some agencies, private and public, that may not accept your homestudy. Therefore it is beneficial to know what placement agency you want to work with before starting your homestudy.

Some people go to a less expensive placement agency after having their homestudy completed elsewhere. Others go to a public/county agency with their homestudy because it is usually inexpensive or free to adopt from a public children services entity.

"Problem Approvals"

Even if you have been approved your assessor can include comments about your interview in the "additional assessor observations" section. These comments may derail a stakeholder from choosing you as an adoptive parent. Your assessor's comments may pertain to any perceived inconsistencies, character concerns, financial statement issues, or other observations. However we have provided you with insider information to lessen the chance of you receiving comments in this section!

Disqualification

Although reasons for denial vary by state, following is a list of the most common reasons applicants are denied the opportunity to adopt:

1. Failure to complete the application for adoption in its entirety.

2. Intentionally supplying false information for the adoption application and/or the homestudy.

3. Failing the safety audit and not willing to make the necessary corrections to pass it.

4. Medical or Psychological documentation that indicates the applicant should not adopt.

5. Conviction of any of the following criminal offenses:

ANIMALS

Cruelty to animals

HOMICIDE

Aggravated murder

Murder

Voluntary manslaughter

Involuntary manslaughter

ASSAULT

Felonious assault

Aggravated assault

Permitting child abuse

Assault

Failing to provide for a functionally impaired person

MENACING

Aggravated menacing

Menacing by stalking

Menacing

PATIENT ABUSE AND NEGLECT

Patient abuse, neglect

KIDNAPPING AND RELATED ISSUES

Kidnapping

Abduction

Child stealing

Criminal child enticement

SEX OFFENSES

Rape

Sexual battery

Unlawful sexual conduct with a minor

Gross sexual imposition

Sexual imposition

Importuning

Voyeurism

Public indecency

Felonious sexual penetration

Compelling prostitution

Promoting prostitution

Procuring

Prostitution

Disseminating matter harmful to juveniles

Pandering obscenity

Pandering obscenity involving a minor

Pandering sexually oriented matter involving a minor

Illegal use of a minor in nudity-oriented material or performance

ARSON

Aggravated arson

Arson

Soliciting or providing support for acts of terrorism

Making a terroristic threat

Terrorism

ROBBERY AND BURGLARY

Aggravated robbery

Robbery

Aggravated burglary

Burglary

THEFT AND FRAUD

Identity Fraud

OFFENSES AGAINST THE PUBLIC PEACE

Inciting to violence

Aggravated riot

OFFENSES AGAINST THE FAMILY

Unlawful abortion

Endangering children

Interference with custody (depending on when the offense occurred)

Contributing to the unruliness or delinquency of a child

Domestic violence

WEAPONS CONTROL

Carrying a concealed weapon

Having a weapon while under disability

Improperly discharging a firearm at or into a habitation or school

DRUG OFFENSES

Corrupting another with drugs

Trafficking in drugs

Illegal manufacture of drugs or cultivation of marijuana

Funding of drug or marijuana trafficking

Illegal administration or distribution of anabolic steroids

Possession of drugs or marijuana that is not a minor drug possession offense

OTHER

Ethnic intimidation

Placing harmful objects in food or confection

Operating a vehicle under the influence of alcohol or drugs – OVI or OVUAC

In some states exceptions to some minor criminal offenses can be made and applicants may be allowed to adopt. Exceptions are rare and you must consult with your state's laws and/ or an attorney for further information.

Please note that you are paying for an assessment, not an approval. Therefore, if your adoption application is denied, you will not be entitled to a refund of your homestudy fee.

Summary:

- All approvals are not created equal. The best type of approval to receive is "approved and recommended."
- Consult with your state and/or an attorney regarding criminal convictions that disqualify applicants from adopting.

Insider Tips:

- Once your agency has approved and finalized your homestudy, you can use it at a different, less expensive agency, including a public agency that charges minimal to no adoption fees.
- A homestudy is an assessment of your suitability to adopt. Because you are paying for an assessment and not an approval, you will not receive a refund of your homestudy fee if your application is denied.

6 THE VAULT

Comments, advice and the secret thoughts of experienced adoption assessors: What they really think about adoptive applicants

"I really want applicants to know that I am not out to get them. I want to approve their homestudy for adoption. Number #1 I like to see children get families, Number #2 I have a financial interst in applicants getting approved. I stand to make more money down the road for other adoption services if they are approved"

"When applicants indicate on the application that they work 60+ hours a week, it looks as if they are workaholics. Sure, they are working to support their lifestyle, but from an adoption perspective it looks as if they won't have enough time to be a good parent. This may not be true, but that's how it's perceived. I hope that they will consider reducing their hours. I know that genetic parents work a lot of hours too. But adoptive parents get scrutinized more for it. It's not fair, but that's the way it is in adoption."

"If someone smokes or allows smoking in their home, as an adoption assessor I'm not really comfortable with putting a child – espically an infant in their home. Considering second hand smoke is known to be associated with a variety of health issues, including asthma, I would not want to put a child in that enviornment. I can't deny someone's homestudy because they smoke, but I would definitely document my concerns in the "additional assessor observations" section, and I would secretly hope that the applicant would quit smoking or that they would not get chosen as an adoptive parent."

"Your pets! Grrrr. Okay, I admit that I am not a pet person. However I do understand that there are some die hard pet lovers out there. My message to you is that not eveyone is a pet lover and not everyone loves your pets like you do. On the other hand their are adoption assessors who love pets. To be sure, ask your assessor if they are okay with pets before they come to your home. If they are not, please volunteer to put them up during the homestudy process."

"Don't over pad your financial statement. I've seen people list limited expenses so it appears that they have more disposable income. Problem is, it was evident that they were omitting expenses because they did not list what they spent on food each month!"

"I prefer that applicants refrain from serving refreshments to me. I realize they think it's the hospitable thing to do, but it puts me in an awkward position because I don't like eating the food of strangers, and I also feel guilty for turning it down. Further, a lot of adoption assessors are social workers and due to professional ethics we are not allowed to accept food, drink or gifts from the customers we serve. It also makes it look as if they are kissing up. It's just best to avoid offering food and drinks altogether."

"It's amazing how perfect marriages become when they are undergoing the scrutiny of the homestudy process. They have no communication issues, they get along perfectly, they love one another's kids from previous marriages, the never get on one another's nerves and the list goes on. I don't believe that for one minute. I'm married, which means I know how trying a marriage can be, even for the best of couples. When a couple tells me that they have no issues I don't believe them. I just wish that applicants would be more real and open about married life."

"When I send a draft of the homestudy to the family for their review, I expect that they will inform me of any spelling or factual errors. I really don't like it when they correct my content, grammar, or sentence structure. In fact, it's quite annoying. Some do it and mean no harm by it. But there are a few who probably do it just to be spiteful."

"I've seen it where applicants have one personality during the homestudy and then a totally different one after they get that approved homestudy. They were putting on during the homestudy so that they could get approved, but then they got kind of mean acting toward me when I had to interact with them post approval. Honestly I think some of the animosity I get from applicants is due to them being secretly resentful about how much it cost to adopt. Either way, I feel duped! And although the homestudy is over, I can and will tell stakeholders about the personality switch I experienced with the applicants."

"There is no need to over-clean your house. I'm only checking to ensure that the home is safe. I think it's funny when I walk into a home and the smell of pine-sol or chocolate chip cookies hits me in the face. I wonder if their home always smells that way."

"If I have to deny someone it is not personal. I'm just abiding by the rules that govern the field of adoption."

"Although I want to help people adopt, I'm more concerned with a child being placed in an appropriate home. Therefore if I suspect that the home might not be safe for a child, I will go the extra mile to investigate the family so that I can be 200% sure that children will be okay in that home."

"The very first time I went to this couple's home, the wife greeted me with a big hug. It was a kind gesture and I understand that she wanted me to feel welcomed. But I really don't like being touched by strangers, so I could have done without that. Further, it clouded my judgment because it was hard to be objective toward such a nice person. I cannot afford to have compromised judgment because children depend on me to ensure they get placed into good homes."

"I was in the middle of a homestudy interview with a couple when the husband pulled out his laptop to watch a football game. He kept it out for the remainder of the interview, and yelled at it when a bad play was made. I was livid and from that point on I could not stand working with this guy. Due to his sheer disrespect I secretly hoped that this couple would not get a child. I had labeled him as an inconsiderate jerk and I got the impression that he was not serious about the homestudy. He just really rubbed me the wrong way. What bothered me even more was that the wife did not ask or **tell** him to put the laptop up! I couldn't tell if she was scared to say something or just plain oblivious. Either way it did not look good. On the surface this looked minor but I'm always assessing the bigger picture when I complete homestudy interviews. I actually started to wonder if she would advocate for her child if her husband was doing something unsafe as it pertained to his parenting. I documented this situation in the "additional assessor observations section.""

"It bothers me when wives talk over their husbands. He is going to be ½ of the parenting equation, so please give him an opportunity to speak during the homestudy interview."

"I've had applicants get snippy with me before their homestudy was even completed and approved. Are you serious? Although I could not deny them for this type of attitude, I can document their attitude in the homestudy. People really need to be more careful with this."

"Before meeting this family (who were non-Latinos) face to face I read on their application that they would accept any race child except a Latino child. After they met me (and saw that I was Latino) they all of a sudden were willing to consider a Latino child. I asked what made them change their mind, and they stated that after reading the trainings they had become more open and comfortable with parenting a Latino child. This could have been true, but because I have been through situations like this with many families I suspect something else was at play. They probably thought that I would hold their original preference against them, considering I was Latino and they did not want a Latino child. Or maybe they realized that it looks bad (or perhaps even racist) to have a paragraph in your homestudy that reads "this family is willing to consider a child from any racial background except Latino. My advice is to be open minded about the type of child you are willing to consider, but to only consider children that you are comfortable with, or are willing to learn more about, so that you can become comfortable with parenting them. Never feel pressured to consider a particular race, or any other demographic trait, just because your assessor belongs to that group of people."

"What bothers me the most are what I call tattle tales. These are clients who you never knew had an issue with the service you provided until you hear it from your boss. It's annoying because I'm in your home for many hours, which presents you with the opportunity to discuss any problems before running to my supervisor.

I applaud people who decide to adopt interracially. Parenting is tough work and it's even more difficult when you are dealing with race or culture related issues. Having said that I think it's sad when I see an African-American child in the store with a non African-American parent, and the child's hair is unkempt. If you are not used to caring for the texture of African-American hair, do seek help so that you can become skilled at this. You can try talking to friends who have experience, or seeking out the services of a professional hair salon until you become proficient. Reading about African-American hair care is not enough. You need to learn how to personally care for it if your child is African-

American, or any other race that has a different hair type than yours."

"I once had an adoptive couple tell me that they were only adopting so that their only biological child could have a sibling. While I think this is a good reason to adopt, I would hope that it is not the only reason. An adopted child needs to be adopted so that they can have a loving and stable family that wanted them for who they are – not just to be a playmate for an existing lonely biological child."

"Just be yourself. Sometimes it seems as if people are putting on a front so that they will be approved to adopt. I see right through that."

"If a family is impatient during the homestudy process, I always wonder how they will fair once it's time to navigate the actual adoption process. The adoption process can be an emotional rollercoaster because it's filled with a lot of waiting and uncertainty. The homestudy is a piece of cake compared to the full blown adoption process."

"People say that they will continue with the adoption process if they happen to get pregnant in the middle of it. But I've seen so many of them put the process on hold if that happens. It's not anything wrong with that, as I can understand that's alot to digest and you need to do what's best for you. However, if prior to the pregnancy you told me that you are all the way adoption, why does that all of a sudden get moved to the back burner when a biological child is conceived? This is why I still believe in my heart of hearts that people value biological children over adopted ones, even when they say they don't."

"If you're adopting a child from a different race, please don't be naïve and think that the world will be color blind and that the child will not be treated differently than you. The world is not color blind, no matter how bad you want to believe that. Because your child may face some race related issues, you should do your best to prepare them for that."

"I know that adoptive parents want their adopted child all to themselves. But it amazes me how un-empathetic they can be toward birthparents at times. They promise the birthparent that they will send pictures for years to come through email so that the birthmother will choose them. But as soon as the adoption finalizes in court, they shut down the email account and stop sending pictures."

"It's an honor to help make sure that children get families. When adoptive families work with me they can be sure they're working with someone who is passionate about their job!"

Homestudy and Adoption Definitions:

Learn the homestudy and adoption definitions that will have you talking like the adoption pros!

Adoption:

A legally recognized process that creates a parent-child relationship between individuals who are not biologically related to each other.

Adoption Agency:

An agency licensed by the state to prepare adoptive parents, counsel birth parents, complete homestudies, complete paperwork, place children in homes, and perform other adoption-related functions.

Adoption Agreement:

The agreement in which the adoptive parent(s) and birthparent(s) put into writing their understanding of the terms of an adoption - including the degree of communication and contact they will have with one other, and/or with the adopted child.

Adoption Plan:

A plan that outlines the wishes of the genetic parents as it pertains to the adoption.

Adoption Professional:

An individual who provides many of the services throughout the adoption process. Typical titles include but are not limited to: adoption assessor, homestudy assessor, adoption worker, social worker, adoption consultant, adoption counselor, and adoption case manager.

Adoption Triangle:

An expression used to describe the inter-relationships among adopted children, their birthparents, and their adoptive parents.

Adoptive Parent:

The mother or father of an adopted child.

At Risk Placement:

The placement of a child into the prospective adoptive family, before the rights of the birthparents have been legally terminated.

Birthparent:

A mother or father who is genetically related to the child.

Certified Copy:

A copy of an official document that has been certified by an official to be authentic and bears an original seal or embossed design.

Closed Adoption:

Adoptions in which the birthparent(s) and the adoptive parent(s) do not meet, do not exchange identifying information, and do not maintain contact with one another post finalization.

Designated Adoption Or Identified Adoption:

An adoption in which the birthparent(s) choose(s) the adoptive parent(s) for the child.

Domestic Adoption:

The adoption of a child born in the United States.

Dossier:

A collection of required documents that is sent to a foreign country in order to process the adoption of a child in that country's legal system.

Facilitator:

A person or organization that encourages and/or arranges domestic and/or international adoptions.

Finalization:

The legal process by which the adoption becomes permanent and binding.

Hague Convention on Intercountry Adoption:

A multi-national agreement designed to promote the uniformity and efficiency of international adoptions.

Homestudy:

A homestudy is an assessment of your family and your readiness to adopt. Your readiness to adopt is determined based on a comprehensive review of your life experiences, health, lifestyle, extended family relationships, attitudes, support system, values, beliefs, and other factors relating to the prospective adoption. This information is summarized and put into one big homestudy report.

Homestudy Agency:

The adoption agency responsible for completing your homestudy.

Independent Adoption:

An adoption arranged privately between the birth family and the adoptive family, without an adoption agency.

Inter-Country Or International Adoption:

The adoption of a child from a different country in which they live.

Non-Identifying Information:

Information that allows the birth and adoptive families to learn pertinent facts about each other without revealing who they are or how they can be contacted.

Open Adoption:

An adoption in which the birthparents and adoptive parents have contact with each other before and/or after the placement of the adopted child.

Post-Placement Services:

A variety of services provided after the adoption is finalized to help ensure that the adoption goes smoothly.

Placement Agency:

The adoption agency responsible for assisting you with adopting a child. This agency may be different than your homestudy agency.

Special Needs Child:

A child with medical, mental, emotional, behavioral, or educational needs that may require extra and on-going attention.

Stakeholders:

Individuals responsible for choosing adoptive parents. They usually include birthparents, adoption agency workers and county social workers.

Termination Of Parental Rights:

The process by which a parent's rights to his or her child are legally and permanently terminated.

U.S. Citizenship and Immigration Services Bureau (USCIS):

An agency of the federal government that approves an adopted child's immigration into the United States and grants U.S. citizenship to children adopted from other countries.

Frequently Asked Questions:

1. What is a homestudy and is it required for all domestic and international adoptions?

A homestudy is an assessment of your family and your readiness to adopt. Your readiness to adopt is determined based on a comprehensive review of your life experiences, health, lifestyle, extended family relationships, attitudes, support system, values, beliefs, and other factors relating to the prospective adoption. This information is then summarized in an adoption homestudy report. A homestudy is required for all adoptions, whether they be domestic or international. The format and cost may vary from state to state and agency to agency, but the general content and the concept of the homestudy is the same everywhere.

2. Is my approved homestudy transferable if I move out of state?

Most states do not have homestudy reciprocity. You must have a homestudy completed by an adoption assessor in the state where you live. Let's say that you live in Ohio and recently had a homestudy completed and approved in Ohio. If you move to Texas and want to be an approved adoptive parent there, you must have a new homestudy completed by an adoption assessor in Texas. Once you have an approved homestudy in Texas, you are free to adopt a child from any state regardless of where you live.

3. Could I have my homestudy completed by one private agency and my adoption completed by different private agency?

Most times you can! It will be at the discretion of the agency. Applicants often do this when they discover that one agency has lower fees than another. The agency that completes your homestudy is your homestudy agency. The agency that is helping you with your adoption is your placement agency. Your placement agency will want to review a copy of your homestudy. Your homestudy agency may or may not request a fee to send the homestudy to them. Before you start working with your homestudy agency ask if they charge a homestudy transfer fee. Fees can vary anywhere from 0-$1000 or more depending on the agency.

4. Is it less expensive to adopt from the county children services division as opposed to adopting privately?

Most times it is significantly less expensive. County adoptions are also known as "state waiting" or "public adoptions". Fees range from free to very minimal costs.

5. Could I use my homestudy completed by a private agency for a public adoption?

Sometimes public agencies will accept homestudies from private agencies. Other times they will require you to complete a new one through them. If you are interested in adopting from a public agency, you should find out their "homestudy reciprocity policy" before hiring any agency to complete your homestudy. This will save you time, money and frustration in the future if the public agency of your choice requires that you complete a homestudy through them.

However, if the public agency of your choice will accept a private agency homestudy, this can save you a ton of money. You could get a homestudy completed quickly through a private agency, and then have that homestudy transferred to a public agency, and pay minimal fees (if any at all) to adopt through their system.

Most times you cannot simply supply the public agency with a copy of your private homestudy. Some public agencies will only accept a copy of your homestudy if it's directly transferred from the agency that completed it.

6. Why do adoption agencies charge fees for amendments and seemingly minor things?

Because they can! Seriously, agencies have to pay their staff for the time that they spend making changes and writing reports. A lot of adoption agencies hire contract workers to complete these tasks. Considering that contract workers are not hourly workers, they charge for everything that they do, i.e. amendments, phone calls, text messages, etc. If you can find an agency that has more hourly employees than contract workers, you may be able to avoid being nickel and dimed for each and every service that you need.

7. I hear that once your homestudy is approved, it could be a very long time before your placement agency finds a child for you to adopt. If this is the case, is there anything else that I could do to find a child quicker?

The timing for birthparent matches vary from state to state and agency to agency. However the common factor in all agency matches is that you have little to no control over how and when your parent profile and/or homestudy is presented to birthparents.

In private agency settings, most times your profile is shown to birthparents in a hard bound book along with the profiles of 5-65 other adopting couples.

The bigger the placing agency, the more hopeful parent profiles they have available.

In the case of public adoptions, your profile is usually viewed by public agency social workers, as parental rights have already been terminated and the child is in the custody of the state. If you're pursuing a public adoption your homestudy and profile may be considered along with 50-60 other hopeful parent profiles. How's that for competition!

In either case the process is antiquated and in a lot of ways overwhelming to birthparents. Birthparents typically meet with agency social workers in a public place and are bombarded with a ton of profiles to review and digest in a short amount of time. Birthparents can take as much time as they need to make a decision, but with so much information to take in at once, they usually just skim through the profiles. What's worse is if they want to take the profiles with them to review later, they have to carry around multiple profiles, and you can only hope that they did not leave yours at a friend's house by mistake or spill coffee on it!

There is a better, more efficient, and super modern way for birthparents to review adoptive parent profiles. If you want more control over the birthparent matching process, additional exposure to birthparents and a way to increase your chances of being chosen, you can try an online profile company such as www.profileconnections.com. This company offers a service that allows you to create an online profile to be viewed by thousands of birthparents across the country. The service also allows you to update your pictures, videos and journals in real time, anytime, from the convenience of your computer! Birthparents can take their time to review profiles and bookmark them to view at a later time. This is done at their leisure and from the comfort of wherever they are.

There is not an agency controlling when, where and how birthparents and adoptive parents connect. If you decide to move forward with an adoption, you can then bring your agency and attorney on board to facilitate the process.

8. Do I have to allow my child to maintain contact with their birthparents after the adoption finalizes in court?

Prior to the adoption finalizing birthparents may request that they receive pictures, emails, phones calls, etc as a way of maintaining contact with the child. If you agree to this before the adoption finalizes, then you should make good on your word. However once the adoption finalizes in court, there are no requirements that you allow this contact to continue - even if you promised it prior to finalization.

9. What if I don't like how my assessor has written my homestudy?

Well, this is a tricky question because you are towing the line of having the right to question this very important document, and needing to accept and respect the assessment completed on your behalf. You should first talk with your assessor about your concerns. They are required to correct objective items such as dates and name spellings. However they are not required to make corrections to their subjective assessment of your family – as this is an assessment based on their professional judgment and years of experience. If you are not satisfied after speaking with your assessor, you can try speaking with their supervisor or the director of the agency.

10. I'm concerned that I have been treated unfairly or discriminated against. What should I do?

The first line of defense would be to speak with you assessor, a supervisor or the agency director. If after taking these steps you are not satisfied with the results, you can file a formal complaint with the state. If you are working with a licensed agency they are most likely licensed and held accountable by the Department of Job and Family Services or a similar entity within your state. Most agencies will supply you with this information before they start working with you.

11. The homestudy process seems so intrusive, why are many the questions very personal and intimate?

This is a very legitimate and good question. It's necessary to ask personal and intimate questions so that the assessor can make an accurate assessment of the family. When an adoption assessor approves and signs off on a homestudy, they are stating that based on their professional judgment and expertise, they believe that the applicant(s) have the fortitude to parent and that a child would be safe, well adjusted and happy in their home. In order to feel confident in making such a statement, the assessor must ask very personal questions to get to know the applicants. Furthermore, if something unfortunate were to ever occur in the home, the courts will question if the family was background checked and sufficiently assessed during the interview. If the answer is "no" to either one of those questions – then the adoption assessor and/or the adoption agency could be held liable for approving the homestudy.

12. Can I receive a refund of the homestudy fee if I am not approved to adopt?

No. When you pay the homestudy fee, you are paying for the homestudy assessment – not an approval. Although you were denied, the assessor still spent many hours completing your homestudy and they have to be paid for their time.

13. What if I change my mind about adopting before the homestudy is complete – will I be issued a refund.

This depends on the agency you are working with and how much of the homestudy was completed. Some agencies may do a pro-rated refund and others may not issue a refund at all. This is a great question to ask your agency prior to starting the homestudy process.

14. Should I ask for a different assessor if I am not clicking with the one assigned to complete my homestudy?

Sure, you can ask for anything that you want! However you may or may not be assigned a new assessor. If the agency is bigger and they have the staff, your wish may be granted. If you're working with a smaller agency your assessor options may be limited. If you decide to request a different assessor – make sure it's for a really good reason. Adoption assessors talk amongst themselves about families, and you could easily be labeled as a "problematic, picky or annoying client."

15. Once I locate an agency that I want to work with, how long will it take before they start and finish my homestudy?

Times vary from agency to agency. In general most agencies will start your homestudy within a few days to a few weeks of receiving your completed application and fee. Expect for it to take anywhere from 2-6 months for your homestudy to be completed. Some agencies offer an expedited homestudy for an additional fee.

RESOURCES

1) Profile Connections: An online community where birthparents and adoptive parents, meet, connect and start the adoption process.

www.profileconnections.com

Services Offered:

- Don't wait on the antiquated agency placement process. Get chosen quicker by posting an electronic profile to be seen by birthparents across the country!

---

2) Homestudybootcamp.com

- Details on the popular book!

3) Social Media

Like our pages on Facebook

Homestudy Boot Camp

Profile Connections

Follow Us on Twitter

@AdoptBabyNow (Homestudy Boot Camp)

@AdoptionProfile (Profile Connections)

Credits

Definitions of religion and spirituality: www.Dictionary.com

Homestudy and Adoption Definitions: Originally published on FindLaw.com, www.findlaw.com

Disqualifying Offenses: Ohio Administrative Code

Front Cover, Back Cover & Spine: Web Lime

VISIT US AT: HOMESTUDYBOOTCAMP.COM